IMAGES
of America

NANTICOKE

IMAGES
of America

NANTICOKE

Chester J. Zaremba

ARCADIA
PUBLISHING

Published by Arcadia Publishing
Charleston, South Carolina

Library of Congress Control Number: 2011923578

For all general information, please contact Arcadia Publishing:
Telephone 843-853-2070
Fax 843-853-0044
E-mail sales@arcadiapublishing.com
For customer service and orders:
Toll-Free 1-888-313-2665

Visit us on the Internet at www.arcadiapublishing.com

*For Cookie, who silently supports my pursuit of the past, and
for Mike, Megan, Tyler, and Braden to whom I leave it*

CONTENTS

ACKNOWLEDGMENTS

The pictures and historical facts contained in this book are from the holdings of the Nanticoke Historical Society. Unless otherwise noted, all images appear courtesy of the Nanticoke Historical Society. Those holdings are from the attics, cellars, old dresser drawers, and shoeboxes of the people who made the history of Nanticoke. From the kind, elderly lady who presented us with a few old black and white pictures to those who shared with us items of their private collections and family archives, we thank you.

The Nanticoke Historical Society (NHS) was formed in 1995, and a special acknowledgement is due for the support given to us in different ways by Martha "Becky" Price, former mayor John Toole, attorney Bernard Kotulak, Barbara Lach, attorney Susan Maza, C. Charles Ciesla, and the late Jule Znaniecki. Znaniecki provided NHS with a substantial amount of photographs, those of which used in this book will be credited as "Znaniecki collection." For Znaniecki's contribution to the preservation of the history of Nanticoke, we are extremely grateful.

The heart of the organization is its members, and the following have gone above and beyond the norm: Mike Passetti, Nick Pucino, Kevin Grevera, Bill and Kathy Sweeney, Barry Littleford, Mike Chmiola, and Dan Chmiola. John Sherrick is undoubtedly the person who knows more about the history of Nanticoke than anyone else today. The detailed work that he has created was used extensively in the development of this book, and without it, the book could not have been written. The glue that holds the organization all together is cofounder and president Julianna Zarzycki. No one works harder, and without her, we would flounder.

Also worthy of our gratitude in sharing their historical photographs are David Sherrick, Dick Kotulak, and Leonard Pawlowski. Sherrick has an extensive collection of Nanticoke memorabilia and has always shared his acquisitions with us. Kotulak was instrumental in providing us with trolley photographs of the late Ed Miller and permission to use them. Pawlowski had provided us with many photographs from the holdings of the former Pawlowski Photo Studio, many of which, contained herein, have only been published once before.

Prior to the establishment of the Nanticoke Historical Society, there was no central repository for the history of Nanticoke. Due to the efforts of those named above, we now have a vibrant, viable organization.

INTRODUCTION

As the coal mining industry came to prominence in Nanticoke, thousands upon thousands of immigrants came here to establish new lives for themselves and their families. The first were the English and Welsh who were experienced in mining operations in their countries. They established the industry, but soon, there was a great need for men to work in the mines and perform the tremendous amount of labor necessary to get the coal to its markets. This second wave of immigration came mainly from the Eastern European countries and, with respect to those settling in Nanticoke, predominately from Poland. Coal breakers and mine shafts appeared and dominated the landscape. As the mining industry thrived, so did Nanticoke, which went from borough to city status in 1924. With a population of 3,884 in 1880, by 1920, there were 22,614 people living in Nanticoke. The population hit its highest point in 1930 when 26,043 were counted in the census of that year. A hospital was established in 1910 to serve the community and, especially, the coal miners who suffered serious injuries on a daily basis. This prosperity led many to build stately and beautiful homes. School buildings of the time were architectural showplaces. The downtown was thriving with stores and shops that fulfilled the need for any material goods. Also thriving were the many bars and saloons that were so much a part of those times.

There were public school buildings in every neighborhood and parochial schools for every Catholic church in Nanticoke. High school sports became a large part of life in the city. The football team won eight conference championships in 14 years, and the Nanticoke High School basketball team won Pennsylvania State Championships in 1923, 1926, and 1961.

Trolleys took us uptown and brought us back to town. They also took us to Sans Souci Park and those memorable school picnics there.

The coal mining industry, which so dominated life in the community, slowly disappeared from the scene. The land on which the Auchencloss operation was located is now a training area for Luzerne County Community College. Susquehanna No. 5 is now a shopping area, and Susquehanna No. 7 has been erased from the landscape.

From about the end of World War II to the late 1950s the area saw the emergence of a large number of garment factories in the city. As the male population was losing jobs due to the decline of anthracite mines, the female population found work in this new industry. But it too saw changes. The overseas manufacturers of clothing were paying their employees wages that were considerably less than the wages being paid here, thus leading to the end of the dress factories.

The Susquehanna River, which first brought the Nentego tribe to our shore, still runs swift and deep. Unfortunately, major flooding in 1936 and again in 1972 brought misery. The Lower Broadway section was able to withstand the flood of 1936, but the devastation of 1972 led to the final demise of "Scalpintown." It has been erased from the landscape.

Gone also are our four movie theaters, the Casino, Family, Rex, and State. Schools, such as Centennial, Pulaski, McKinley, West Main Street, State Street, Garfield, Washington, Kosciuszko, and Main Street, are gone. They have been erased.

But in the midst of the erasures, the city lives on and rebuilds. It lives on each day going about its business and continuing to make history. It lives on in the pictures in our minds and on the following pages.

One

CHANGES

As the pioneer settlers began to establish themselves in what is now Nanticoke, they were a farming community and set up gristmills at the Nanticoke Falls, which was actually the rapids area of the river. In addition to farming, shad fishing in the Susquehanna was lucrative. In the "Great Haul of 1789," an estimated 10,000 shad were landed at Nanticoke. But changes were coming; coal was discovered. Col. Washington Lee set up the first coal mine in the hillsides of Honey Pot in 1825. Coal was taken from the mines and hauled down to the river and loaded into barges for shipment to markets south of here. The coal mining industry flourished, and it brought with it tremendous prosperity to Nanticoke. A building boom was on, and the population grew. The city thrived, and the times were good, but as the world turned from coal to other sources of energy, it brought changes. The mines began to close, and people moved away seeking other employment. The face of Nanticoke began to change. The proliferation of the automobile brought mobility to the people; shopping was no longer confined to Nanticoke, and stores began to close. As the city began to fall into a state of deterioration, redevelopment emerged to rescue it. Changes were again coming; this time, they were for the better. Dilapidated buildings were demolished, and new construction took place. Homes were rehabilitated or removed, new schools replaced the old, and new roadways were built, and the city once more adapted to these changes.

Throughout all the changes, Nanticoke has remained a good place to live and raise a family. Those who have served in city government have always found a way to get the job done in spite of monumental financial difficulties. The police and fire departments continue to change with the times and provide exceptional around-the-clock service. Changes in any community are inevitable, and Nanticoke has handled them well. In order to better deal with future changes, one must examine those that have already occurred.

1. PUBLIC SCHOOLS.
2. HOTEL BROADWAY. D. B. WILLIAMS PROP.
3. WERNET HOUSE. J. H. OPLINGER "
4. GRIST MILL. W. B. FREAS & SON "
5. MINING DRILL WORKS. FRED. T. BITTENBENDER
6. P. R. R. STATION.
7. C. R. R. of N. J. STATION.
8. OPERA HOUSE.
9. SUSQUEHANNA COAL CO. BREAKER No. 1.
10. —————— " —————— " —————— " No. 2.
11. —————— " —————— " —————— SHAFT "
12. —————— " —————— " —————— SLOPE "
13. —————— " —————— " —————— SEPARATER "

NANT
PENN

Thaddeus Fowler produced nearly 200 bird's-eye-view maps for towns throughout Pennsylvania. In his 1890 view of Nanticoke, it can be seen that the basic layout of the town is already in place. There is a covered bridge across the Susquehanna River, and coal-mining operations dominate the landscape. Rail lines that will serve the anthracite industry for the next 70 years are in place.

COKE,

ANIA

A. ST. FRANCIS ROMAN CATHOLIC CHURCH
B. ST. STANISLAUS POLISH " "
C. HUNGARIAN " " "
D. " CHURCH.
E. GERMAN LUTHERAN.
F. PRESBYTERIAN CHURCH
G. EPISCOPAL
H. "
I. WELSH CONGREGATIONAL "
J. WELSH M. E.
K. " BAPTIST "
M. ENGLISH " "
N. WELSH CONGREGATIONAL. "

Rows of identical coal company homes lined Slope, Hill, and Coal Streets. These homes were rented from the company for $3.50 a month, and a number of them still exist. Room for expansion around the town is abundant. This 111-year-old glimpse of Nanticoke shows that by 1890 it was a well-established, vibrant community with infrastructure.

11

A large parade was held as part of Chautauqua Week, July 15–21, 1914. Chautauqua gatherings provided entertainment, cultural speeches, and related events to communities. The first Chautauqua in Luzerne County was held at Nanticoke in 1913 at Dietrick's Field in Dewey Park. The 1914 event was unable to be held at that previous location, as ground had just been broken there for the new high school building. It was therefore moved to a location, which eventually became Lincoln Field. (Courtesy of Znaniecki collection.)

This 1904 view of Main Street shows the proliferation of telephone lines in the downtown business district. At this time in the development of the telephone, it was necessary to run one line from the pole to each individual phone. Although trolley service was available, horse-drawn wagons were still the main means of transportation. (Courtesy of William Horn.)

12

Main Street, Nanticoke, Pa.

This is a view of Main Street when life seemed to be much more quiet and serene. A horse with buggy trots down the street, while a trolley enters the picture on the left. The dresses worn by the ladies on the right were most likely their everyday, going-to-town attire.

Pannebecker   Nanticoke, Pa.

This turn-of-the-century photograph of a Nanticoke family was taken at the Pannebecker Photo Studio, which was located on the third floor of 122 East Main Street. Samuel Pannebecker established his photography business in 1884 and continued in his work until his death in 1918. During that time, the majority of Nanticoke families and individuals had their studio photographs done at Pannebecker's.

13

Prior to the arrival of the automobile as a personal means of transportation, a large number of local "traction" companies existed to serve local areas. One of these was the Nanticoke-Newport Electric Railway Company, which ran only that route, from Nanticoke to Newport. Car No. 3 is an early example of organized and reliable transportation. It ran on rails and was powered by a single overhead wire.

This undated photograph shows the Singer Sewing Machine Company float in front of 588 East Main Street prior to a Fourth of July parade. Singer Sewing Machine agents included the Hildreth Store at 2–6 North Market Street in 1894, P. Edmunds at 21 West Green Street, and B.F. Griffith at 186 South Market Street in 1910. (Courtesy of Znaniecki collection.)

As the years progressed into the late 1910s and early 1920s, changes came about in the way of the addition of new stores and businesses along with repairs and improvements to the Main Street. In this photograph, only one horse and wagon can be seen, as the automobile begins its domination of the streets.

This classic postcard view of East Main Street shows the new look of the town, as all the old telephone poles are gone and the wires have been placed underground. This view of the downtown area remained the same for many years until the business area began to fade and stores began to close.

Here is a slightly different postcard view of the Main and Market Streets area with no vehicular traffic. It can be seen that the roadway is paved with brick. The building on the left in this photograph fell to redevelopment in the late 1950s, whereas the buildings and storefronts on the right lasted well into the 1990s. That area is now occupied by the Rite-Aid Pharmacy store.

Changes continued, which can be seen in this 1947 photograph. Well-established businesses, such as Leventhal's Men's Clothing and Triangle Shoes and People's Shoe Store, anchor the downtown. Leventhal's is offering Adam hats at $2.95. The trolley has arrived in town; however, it appears that the snowplow has not. (Ed Miller Photograph.)

Market St. South from Main, Nanticoke, Pa.

This postcard view of the Main Street and Market Street intersection shows the newly constructed L.C. Gabriel Building, which was first used as a meat market in 1909. Gabriel later established a saloon there, and the building eventually became the Nanticoke Hotel. A look up South Market Street shows that development of that area is just beginning.

The Strauss Furniture Store is shown prominently in this 1930 look down Main Street. Philip Strauss was known as "the ideal American merchant" by the late 1920s. When he arrived in Wilkes-Barre from Austria in 1894, he was a young orphaned boy. He found work, went to night school, and saved his money. In 1909, he became manager of a Nanticoke store; 10 years later, with $10,000, he opened his own "Million Dollar Store."

A large crowd awaits the arrival of the Six County Fireman's Association convention parade in 1953. Behind the crowd are the stores that comprised the business district at this point in time. William E. Davis was the fire chief at the time of this convention. Other Six County Fireman's Association conventions and parades were held in Nanticoke in 1929, 1963, and 1993.

This view of North Market Street looking south was taken just prior to the beginning of the area's redevelopment, which resulted in the demolition of all of these buildings with the exception of the post office on the southwest corner of the Main Street and Market Street intersection. Just visible on the left side of this photograph is the Cease Motors Company, a Dodge and Plymouth automobile dealership. The area on the extreme right of the photograph is now the location of the US Post Office. (Courtesy of Norm Borofski.)

A memorable view of Nanticoke's Main Street is shown in this remarkable photograph. It is one of the last pictures taken of the original layout of stores and buildings at the Main Street and Market Street intersection looking east. The buildings on the right stand as they did since the 1920s and 1930s and as they would until the 1990s. The buildings on the left would fall to the wrecking ball to make way for new development. This photograph was taken around 1959. (Courtesy of Norm Borofski.)

In contrast to the prior photograph, this picture shows the beginning of the decline of the downtown business district. The buildings on the left are awaiting demolition, while some of the stores that lined the right side of Main Street in this block are going out of business. The sign in Albert's states, "Going out of business, leaving town," and the sign in the window of Gordon's relates the news that it is closing after having been in business for 38 years. (Courtesy of Norm Borofski.)

By 1979, the classic view of Main Street shows new buildings housing the Rea and Derick Drugstore and the Leventhal's Men's Clothing Store. Some stores along the south side remain open, while a few are empty. A late 1990s redevelopment project led to the demolition of all those stores to make way for the construction of a Rite-Aid Pharmacy.

Although the face of the Borough and City of Nanticoke has changed over the last century, the service and dedication of the men and women of the fire and police departments has not. They have continually strived to have the latest in equipment and technology to perform their duties. At the turn of the 20th century, the Hanover Hose Company No. 4 acquired this newly developed four-wheel, horse-drawn fire wagon. It is pictured here in front of the Hotel Broadway. (Courtesy of Znaniecki collection.)

M.F. Coons O.P.O. Dry Goods store and R. Raphael's Clothing store were completely gutted by fire on Sunday, August 19, 1906. The total loss was over $60,000 and was called the worst fire in Nanticoke since the 1870s. At 1:15 a.m., the alarm was sounded and Stickney Hose Company responded. When the extent of the fire was discovered, four other companies were called out. Before the fire was finally extinguished, Chief Daniels and his men worked from 1:20 until 7:50 a.m. The Robert Schwartz wholesale liquor business and dwelling next to the Raphael Building also took fire, but this fire was quickly brought under control. The spaces between these joists acted as flues, and the flames were drawn through them to the top of the building so that the roof and basement were on fire, while the floors between did not catch until later. The cellars were so flooded that no one could enter them and the exact spot where the fire started could not be learned. While the Raphael family succeeded in escaping uninjured, they were unable to save anything.

In 1929, members of the Lape Hose Company posed for this formal photograph outside of their station at Broad and Walnut Streets. The company was formed in 1884 and was originally named the Union Fire Company No. 2 or "the Rough and Ready." It was later renamed in honor of Alvin A. Lape, the first fire chief.

The Stickney Fire Company, shown here in 1938, was the first fire company organized in Nanticoke. It is named in honor of Joseph Stickney, chief executive of the Susquehanna Coal Company who helped to organize it. Originally housed in an old barn in the rear of West Main Street, it was subsequently moved to Prospect Street, shown here, in 1912. (Courtesy of Nanticoke Fire Department.)

In 1886, David S. Williams and Gomer D. Lewis organized the Pioneer Hook and Ladder Company. The first hook and ladder was pulled by hand. Because of the hilly terrain of Nanticoke, the firemen would be exhausted by the time they arrived at the scene of a fire. This photograph shows their 1933 truck in front of their building at Broad and Walnut Streets.

The Union Engine Company was organized on May 21, 1888, to give protection to the south or "back of the hill" section. It was a long climb for firemen downtown to pull a hand-drawn, two-wheel horse cart up dirt streets. In 1889, the name was changed to A.K. Mowery Hose Company. This photograph shows the new building on Noble Street and the company's 1924 LeFrance pumping engine. (Courtesy of Nanticoke Fire Department.)

First organized in 1876, this 1908 police photograph includes, from left to right, (first row) Chief Ford, Mayor Cooney, and George Smith; (second row) Officers Kocikowski, Wint, Jones, and Gorka. Also in that year, Gorka came upon two men driving a cow along Main Street. When the men could not prove ownership of the cow, he took possession of it and began to care for it at his home. The rightful owner was eventually found. (Courtesy of Nanticoke Police Department.)

Mayor Evan J. Williams is shown with the Nanticoke Police Department of 1932; members had just received new uniforms. In that year, the police department vehicles consisted of a 1916 and a 1923 Dodge truck, a 1932 Chevrolet sedan, and a 1927 Indian motorcycle. In 1932, Anthony Pilarek and Stanley Rasmus served as chiefs of police. (Courtesy of Nanticoke Police Department.)

The American Automobile Association (AAA) began the School Safety Patrol Program in 1920. In 1933, Pres. Franklin D. Roosevelt commented that in addition to the day-to-day prevention of accidents, the patrol was a builder of morale and it developed a sense of responsibility in its members. Police chief Vincent Znaniecki and officer Joseph Magnosi honored the Nanticoke School Safety Patrol members in 1934. (Courtesy of Znaniecki collection.)

Draftees from Nanticoke prepare to board a train. Capt. Robert F. Waters received word on April 6, 1917, to recruit up to 145 men. Local newspapers called for the young men of the nation to volunteer their services. Of the recruits volunteering for Battery C, many were found to be unfit for military duty. The names of those who were rejected were often published in the *Wilkes-Barre Record*, much to their embarrassment.

A massive crowd gathered at the Nanticoke Train Station in 1919 to welcome home the men who served and fought in World War I. Seen in the photograph next to the station are buildings of the Susquehanna Brewing Company. In the background, the No. 5 breaker of the

Susquehanna Coal Company is visible. Note that horses and buggies are still the dominate means of transportation.

A mammoth parade was held on August 21, 1919, for returning World War I veterans. Temporary wooden archways to welcome home the men were constructed on Main Street at Prospect Street, as shown here, and also in front of the Mill Estate on East Main Street. This photograph also shows the Casino Theatre at Main and Prospect Streets. On October 29, 1919, this welcome arch was damaged by high winds and was taken down the same day so as not to pose a danger to the public.

Two

SALES AND SERVICES

As Nanticoke grew, so did its need for goods and services. Early commercial enterprises accommodated the needs of the day. Just as in every other community, there were blacksmiths, harness makers, wheelwrights, and millers. As time moved on and needs changed, general stores emerged but soon gave way to businesses that were specific in nature to one product or service. The First National Bank of Nanticoke went into business on January 14, 1889, and offered loans to those who wished to set up a business at that time. Hotels, such as the Hotel Broadway, the Wernet House, and the Nanticoke Hotel, offered in addition to clean rooms, the use of its dining facilities, poolrooms, and reading and writing rooms. Samuel H. Kress and his business partner Dr. Harter established a stationery store at 8 North Market Street in 1884. Dr. Harter later withdrew from the business, and Kress became a multimillionaire after he founded the S.S. Kresge Company, a national chain of retail stores. Another major business was the Fairchild Ice Company, which existed until 1937. Ice was cut from local ponds and stored in the icehouse at 162 Hanover Street, the family residence. Emil Malinowski started in business at Main Street and Broadway repairing wagons and mine machinery. He went on to found the Franklin Brewery and the Miners Bank and Trust. He was Nanticoke's second millionaire. Remembering that the 1920 population of Nanticoke was over 22,000, consider the fact that the 1919 business register lists 160 grocery stores. It also states that there were 160 taverns, an issue that will be covered in a following chapter.

The Nanticoke business community thrived well into the pre-mall, mid- to late 1950s. A typical trip to town back then could have started with a quick bite to eat at Nardozzo's or Gayson's, followed by a stop at Berman's to buy the latest 45 rpm record and pick up a copy of the WARM Top 40 sheet, continued on with visits to Woolworth's and Newberry's, and concluded with a slow walk home. A person could get almost anything one wanted in Nanticoke.

In one of Nanticoke's earliest commercial endeavors, David Williams operated a truck farm on the Nanticoke Flats between Dewey Park and Dundee. At the turn of the 20th century, he sold his produce from this horse-drawn wagon. The dirt street and the grandeur of the homes in the background are noteworthy. (Courtesy of Znaniecki collection.)

This building at 122 East Main Street was photographed on October 12, 1904, immediately prior to a parade to celebrate the opening of the Nanticoke Hospital. The Pannebecker Photo Studio was located on the third floor, and there was a grocery on the ground level. Immediately to the right was Allen's Confectionery Store.

Andrew Kopcho operated a meat market at 226 Front Street in the Hanover section of Nanticoke from 1919 until 1927. He is shown on the right with an unidentified employee. The Hanover section had a number of stores along Front Street to serve the people of that area.

This building along front street, in a somewhat dilapidated condition, was purchased around 1919 by Andrew Lakatos who then had it remodeled and opened a general store. This building still serves as a commercial establishment at the present time. (Courtesy of Helen Buczkowski.)

Small neighborhood grocery stores dotted the landscape in the 1950s prior to the advent of the grocery supermarket. In addition to groceries, Del Wolever sold greeting cards at his store on the corner of East Green and Chestnut Streets. (Courtesy of Nanticoke Redevelopment Authority.)

In this 1908 photograph, Karol Guszkiewicz (left) and another man are standing in front of his meat market at the corner of College and Church Streets. William J. Treymayne purchased this building in 1923 when he opened a grocery store there. His son Donald F. Treymayne took over the business in 1952, and it continued in operation until 1969. It is currently the site of Larry's Pizza, a well-known city business.

Here is a turn-of-the-20th-century photograph of the interior of the Brinton Jackson grocery store at 108 Prospect Street. Jackson, standing directly under the moose head in the photograph, served a term as Luzerne County prothonotary and also served as the president of the First National Bank of Nanticoke. A native of Kennett Square near Philadelphia, he is buried there in the family plot. (Courtesy of Znaniecki collection.)

Newspaper boys pose with their wagons advertising Scureman's Cheerups, a confectionary product manufactured by Joseph B. Scureman at this store at 8–10 East Main Street. Shortly after this c. 1913 photograph, he moved the store to 42 East Main Street where he conducted business until 1929. William Anthony purchased the store from him upon his retirement and subsequent move to California. (Courtesy of Znaniecki collection.)

Franciszek Szczuka was born in Poland in 1875 and came to Nanticoke in 1883 to work in the coal mines as Frank Stooks. After a few years in the mines, he established a grocery store at 17 West Main Street and is pictured here with his wife, Helen. The boy and the dog are unidentified. (Courtesy of Znaniecki collection.)

Frank Stooks is shown in the interior of his store. Customer's groceries were delivered to their home by his horse and wagon, an innovative idea in 1895. He served a term as treasurer in the Borough of Nanticoke and was also the secretary of the Nanticoke Polish Alliance Society. (Courtesy of Znaniecki collection.)

Frank Stooks died in 1927, and so his children ran the business. In another later view of the store's interior, Frank's daughter Helen is shown taking care of business. The man in the photograph is unidentified. (Courtesy of Znaniecki collection.)

From 1936 to 1937, the interior of the store was totally remodeled, resulting in a new, modern look. At the same time, Helen Stooks took over management. The building was demolished in 1969 to make way for the Carroll's Drive-in Restaurant. (Courtesy of Znaniecki collection.)

In 1911, Felix Dombrowski purchased the Cooney Cigar Store, shown here, at 43 South Market Street and set up his jewelry business. Out of this store, he also sold newspapers in various languages, tobacco, magazines, and sheet music. (Courtesy of Stephanie Dombrowski Zimolzak.)

Felix Dombrowski moved his jewelry store to 32 South Market Street in 1916. Standing in front of the new location are, from left to right, Elenore Dombrowski, Felix Dombrowski, and store clerk Sophia Stooks, daughter of Frank and Helen Stooks. (Courtesy of Stephanie Dombrowski Zimolzak.)

Pictured is the interior of Woolworth's five-and-dime store at 1 North Market Street. The amount and variety of merchandise is outstanding. The signs above the counters advise the customer that the items are for sale for either a nickel or a dime.

The Thompson brothers, Leonard, Frank, John, and Sidney, pose with their Thompson Brothers Express trucks, which were contracted to the American Railway Express Company. This 1919 photograph was taken in front of the Nanticoke Passenger Rail Station in the vicinity of Arch and Railroad Streets, which was where the Thompson brothers had their office.

This building at 547 South Walnut and Ridge Streets was constructed in 1908 by Frank Rokosz who operated a grocery store and an electrical appliance store there. The appliance store was known as Voss Sales. His fleet of service and delivery trucks is seen parked outside in this 1925 photograph. (Courtesy of Znaniecki collection.)

Members of the Rokosz family pose along side of two delivery trucks, which carry signs reading, "Mrs. P. Rokosz and Sons, Distributors of Voss Washing Machines." Pearl Rokosz also ran another store at 102 South Market Street at the time. (Courtesy of Znaniecki collection.)

George Perluke poses with his truck in front of the Wesley Auto Garage on Broadway. He ran a successful ice delivery business for many years in the Hanover section of Nanticoke. Eventually, the ice business gave way to a cooperage operation near Mosier Street. (Courtesy of William Zaremba.)

The Znaniecki brothers' service station at 500 East Main Street was the first drive-in gas station in Nanticoke. This building was constructed in 1928 and operated as a service center well into the early 1960s. Vincent Znaniecki also served as chief of police and mayor of the City of Nanticoke, and his wife, Jule Znaniecki, was well known for her historical research. (Courtesy of Znaniecki collection.)

Frank F. Matheson was the president of the automobile firm bearing his name. In 1905, the Matheson automobile plant moved from New England to Forty Fort, Pennsylvania. Frank Matheson was the distributor for Pontiac and Oakland motorcars in Luzerne County. Grand opening of the Nanticoke branch's showroom and service station, located on the corner of West Main and North Market Streets, took place on September 18, 1926.

In this view of the Matheson's automobile showroom, new cars can be seen on the sales floor. In 1932, the US government purchased the property for the construction of a post office. Prior to its use by Matheson, the building housed the McWilliams Department Store.

In 1934, Peter Bartuska Sr. and his wife, Anna, opened a sewing shop at 200 East Main Street. He specialized in repairing and selling new and used sewing machines. Later, he expanded his business to be more of a general store–type operation, selling furniture, appliances, radios, toys, and flooring. (Courtesy of Denis and Jim Bartuska.)

Peter Bartuska eventually took on the Singer Sewing Machine line when that company moved out of the building. In the 1950s, he became a television dealer, and with the help of his son Peter Jr., they brought television for the first time to many Nanticoke residents. The store remains in operation today with grandsons Denis and Jim heading the operation. (Courtesy of Denis and Jim Bartuska.)

Bruce Janoski is shown here with two of his daughters in front of his new store at 131 South Market Street. He began as a businessman in 1909 and was a partner in the Janoski Brothers Picture and Frame business on Main Street. He constructed this building in 1921 and began selling wallpaper and paint. The business continued into the 1960s, and the building still stands at that address.

Stanley Janosczyk's Quality Meat Market was located at 396 East Ridge Street. Alex Ftorkowski had a shoe-repairing business on the College Street side of the building. Noteworthy is the fact that College Street is paved, while Ridge Street and the sidewalks around the business are still dirt. (Courtesy of Janosczyk family.)

In 1919, Jones's Boston Store at 11 East Main Street and O'Brien's Drugstore at 15 East Main Street were vacated, and the space was made into the J.J. Newberry's five-and-dime store. It was the archetypical department store where almost anything could be purchased. It continued its successful business run well into the 1960s. (Pawlowski Photograph.)

In this close-up view of the left-hand window of Newberry's, a display of telephones announces the change in Nanticoke telephone numbers in 1960. The Regent name was to be used in front of Nanticoke numbers, which by this point in time had exceeded 6,000. The Regent prefix was short lived, giving way to the digits 73 in its place. (Pawlowski Photograph.)

Harry Cimmet came to Nanticoke at age 25 and opened a general notions store at 5 East Main Street. Cimmet's Sterling Variety Store became known for having hard-to-find items not available elsewhere. The business was passed on to his sons Harold and Isadore who continued it until the 1970s. Isadore was captured and made a prisoner of war during World War II's Battle of the Bulge but was able to return to Nanticoke after his release. (Pawlowski Photograph.)

A display window at the Gem Furniture Store at 154 South Market also advertises the new telephones as the number change was occurring. Frank S. Boguszewski first operated his National Floor Covering Store in 1924 and later founded the Gem Furniture Store at the Market Street address. In 1935, the National Floor Covering store combined with the Gem Furniture store, and the two continued business as one on Market Street. (Pawlowski Photograph.)

Joseph's Furniture Store, owned and operated by Joseph J. Grzymski, is shown here at its North Market Street location immediately prior to the property being acquired for demolition by the redevelopment authority. In 1962, Grzymski moved his store to the building formerly occupied by the Strauss Furniture Store on East Main Street.

The Leader Store was founded by William D. Jenkins in 1917. Noteworthy to this store was its unique ceiling track system. The store clerks were not required to handle any money transactions. The clerk would write out a bill, accept payment, and send it via a carrying car to the office on the balcony, and a receipt and change would then be returned by the same means to the customer.

The inside display window of the Leader Store is decorated for Easter in these undated photographs. The window on the left is the freestanding display island, which was located between the two front doors. (Pawlowski Photograph.)

The stairs leading down to the bargain basement can be seen on the right in this interior view. The track system can be clearly seen along the ceiling, with spurs of it dropping down to the sales counters. The Leader Store was the largest department store in Nanticoke. (Pawlowski Photograph.)

The ceiling track system, as it leads to the balcony area of the store in the rear, can also be seen in this interior view. A cashier who handled all money transactions was stationed in the balcony. (Pawlowski Photograph.)

The main display window of the Leader Store was always professionally decorated, as it is shown here for the new spring fashions. The neighboring bank purchased the Leader Store, had it demolished, and enlarged its operation by constructing an addition to the main bank building. (Pawlowski Photograph.)

F.M. Kirby established his five-and-dime store in Nanticoke in 1909 and in 1913 changed the name to F.W. Woolworth Company. In 1941, he purchased the Lew Levi Clothing Store at 30 East Main Street and moved his business there after extensive renovation of that property. The building later became the home of the CVS Pharmacy. (Pawlowski Photograph.)

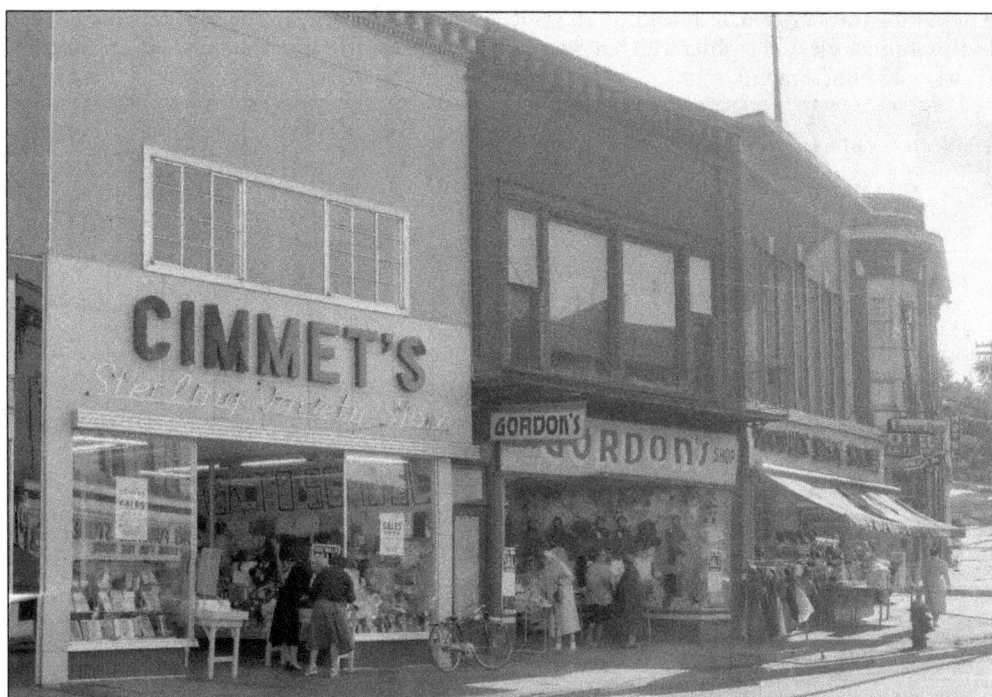

This is an excellent view of Cimmet's, Gordon's, and People's Shoe Store in 1960 when they all had thriving businesses. Details in the photograph, such as the boy's bicycle and the lady shopper wearing a babushka, add local color. (Pawlowski Photograph.)

Joseph Elinski founded the Noble Furniture Store at 23–25 East Noble Street in Nanticoke in 1947. In 1969, a devastating fire totally destroyed the building shown here. The store was eventually relocated to the 800 block of East Main Street and is now actually in Hanover Township. It continues to be run by members of the Elinski family today.

Henry W. Lark began the first radio station in Nanticoke in 1946 on the third floor of the Lew Levi Clothing Store on Main Street. He chose the call letters WHWL based on his initials. The station broadcast its signal at 730 on the AM band. In 1960, Lark sold the station to attorney Martin Phillips who changed the call letters to WNAK. This photograph shows an Amphicar, which was used as a promotional vehicle for the station. The Amphicar is a German-made amphibious automobile capable of 70 miles per hour on land and seven knots in the water. The vehicle is parked in front of the Lincoln School on Kosciuszko Street around 1965. (Edward A. Sadowski Photograph.)

In 1914, E. Bixby Wesley established a Ford dealership as the Wesley Auto Company at 134 Broadway. In 1927, one of his newspaper advertisements stated that he was the oldest Ford dealership in Wyoming Valley. This promotional photograph for the 1940 Mercury automobile shows the front of the Wesley Auto Company. (Courtesy of Znaniecki collection.)

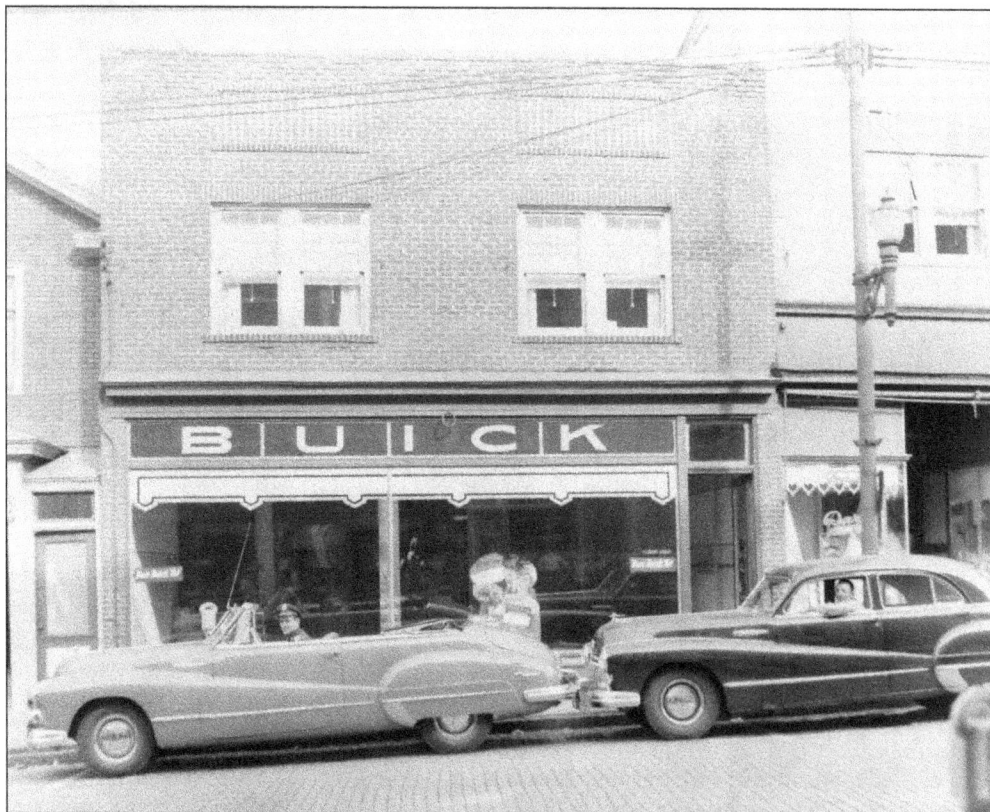

Two new 1948 Buicks are seen in front of the Albert Rees Buick Dealership at 183 Market Street in this promotional photograph. The dealership was started in 1915 by Albert Rees and was later taken over by his son Carl Rees. Carl ran the business until 1970, when he sold it to John Krop. Teddy Osmanski's Park Cigar Store, generally known as "the Smoke Shop," can be seen immediately to the right of the Rees Building. (Pawlowski Photograph.)

This postcard view of Walnut and State Streets shows why this area was home to some of Nanticoke's most prominent citizens in the 1920s. St. John's Lutheran Church can be seen in the background. Homes on State Street have a view overlooking the downtown area, the Nanticoke Flats, and the Susquehanna River.

A nighttime view of the Al Fink Oldsmobile dealership on West Main Street provides an excellent view of the new cars on the showroom floor. Both Oldsmobiles are 1948 models. (Pawlowski Photograph.)

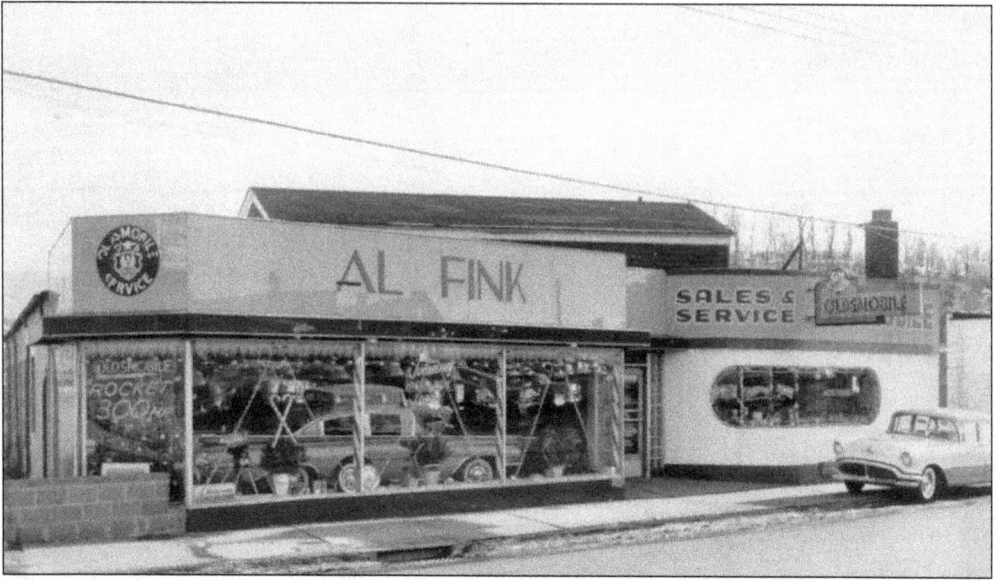

With Christmas decorations in the windows, the Al Fink Oldsmobile dealership has a 1959 Oldsmobile on the showroom floor for sale. A 1956 Oldsmobile is parked along the sidewalk. The building is in use today as a recycled building materials store. (Pawlowski Photograph.)

When coming in to or going out of town, one passed Eddie Janison's fruit stand. This was the view in 1958 just prior to the construction of a large retail store at 575 East Main Street. Janison grew much of his produce in the immediate area, which ensured super freshness. (Courtesy of Sandra Janison Dungey.)

Three

BUILDINGS AND HOMES

People learned how to live their lives in their houses, their churches, their schools, and their workplaces. What they learned in those buildings is always brought back to mind when they look at them from the outside. They remember the warmth of those houses, the grandeur of the churches, and the stateliness of the schools. When they lose those buildings, they lose a little part of themselves. While the buildings still stand, they believe that they can reenter them and return to those wonderful days of yesteryear. But for most part, they cannot. Those wonderful places live on only in their memories and in the pages of a book.

For those living in Nanticoke, they liked what they had and thought it would be that way forever. But, the buildings were getting old and redevelopment was moving in. Stores that used to be filled with customers were the first to go, followed by a large number of dilapidated houses, but the community was still pretty much intact as far as memories go. Then, they started to take things that hurt. They took the junior high school; they took the State Theatre. Then, they took the high school. For two weeks, it fought the wrecking ball, but in the end, it fell. Many were there for that final fall, a fall that took with it any chance for many to return to yesteryear.

People will go back, however, back to the way Nanticoke was, the way they remember it. These buildings were one of a kind. For many reasons, they could never be duplicated today. They may be gone, but really, they are still with Nanticoke in many ways.

In 1896, it was decided to use this building as city hall as well as the home for the Pioneer Hook and Ladder Company. During the 1905 typhoid fever epidemic, it was set up as an emergency hospital as the Nanticoke Hospital was not yet in existence. The Lape Hose Company moved into this building in 1910. Facilities were shared between the Lape and Pioneer companies until the consolidation of all fire companies at a central headquarters. (Courtesy of Znaniecki collection.)

In January 1911, the borough council authorized the expenditure of $16,000 for the construction of a new "city building." The new building was to be placed on the site of the former Lape Hose Company. On June 13, 1911, the borough council held its first meeting in its new building. The borough police department and jail were also located in this structure, which was replaced by the current city building.

The Nanticoke Municipal Building is located at 15 East Ridge Street and houses all government offices. Ground was broken for this $632,000 building in January 1973. The building was dedicated on February 16, 1975. The historical marker on the lawn of the municipal building was once located at the intersection of Main and Kosciuszko Streets. Weather worn and faded due to its age, it was restored by the Nanticoke Historical Society.

The Susquehanna Coal Company Building stood for 100 years. With construction started in 1910, it was first occupied on May 1, 1911. The doors were unique in that the left-side door led onto the first floor of the building, while the right-side door opened to a stairway leading to the second floor. The concrete "Susquehanna Coal Company" header has been preserved and is in the possession of the Nanticoke Historical Society.

A building that was very prominent in the early history of Nanticoke was the Broadway Opera House, which was later known as the Broadway Armory. This building was constructed in 1887 on the site of a former opera house that was destroyed by fire. The seating capacity was 1,400, and it was the site of many theatrical plays and even an indoor baseball game at one time. In 1911, it was converted to a National Guard Armory by the state. (Courtesy of Tony Diksa.)

Today's antique collectors can find old beer bottles, old beer trays, and advertisements from the Susquehanna Brewing Company. The enterprise operated from this building on Alden Road from the late 1880s until the structure was demolished in 1940. The bottling house building still stands at the Alden Road and West Main Street intersection.

This is a 1916 view of the Oplinger Hotel at Market and Spring Streets. It was owned and operated by Galen Oplinger, the son of John Oplinger, who ran the Oplinger Hotel—also known as the Wernet House—on Main Street.

Charles Hesser's hotel at the corner of Locust Street and 33 East Main Street began as Xavier Wernet's Hotel and Wernet's Fountain House. Hesser purchased the building from Wernet in 1907, renamed it the Hotel Hesser, and sold it to Jerome O'Brien in 1914. Despite changing hands several times thereafter, it continued to be known as the Hesser. (Courtesy of Znaniecki collection.)

The First National Bank of Nanticoke was started in a storefront in 1888. A new building, shown here at its opening, was constructed in 1903. By 1912, it was decided to rebuild the facade of the bank, and this ornate front was replaced by a more modern look. Throughout its history, the First National Bank was one of the strongest in the country regarding surplus and capital.

The new 1912 facade of the First National Bank was modern and clean in its appearance. The renovations included marble walls and counters, solid bronze grillwork, glass desks in the lobby, and floors of Tennessee marble. The building still stands today, although, it is not used for any purpose other than storage, but upon close examination, one can catch a glimpse of its former grandeur.

The Nanticoke National Bank was chartered in 1904 and constructed its iconic building in 1912 on the site of the Hotel Hesser at Main and Locust Streets. To facilitate this, the Hotel Hesser was moved a distance up Locust Street to make way for the bank. This building is finished in 500 tons of gray Vermont granite. The main vault weighs 27 tons and is surrounded by two feet of concrete reinforced with nickel-steel.

Peoples Trust Company was established in 1921 at 74 East Main Street. The building at that site was the Nanticoke Drug Company, located in a two-story brick structure, which was purchased by Peoples Trust and remodeled into the banking facility at a cost of $80,000 in 1923. It later became Peoples National Bank and merged with First Eastern Bank in 1986. This structure was demolished to make way for an office building in the early 1990s.

In 1895, Joseph Stickney, chief executive of the Susquehanna Coal Company, organized the Stickney Fire Company. In 1912, the Stickney Fire Company took possession of its building at 24 Prospect Street and began fundraising projects to pay for furnishings and the new $5,792 Seagraves engine. It was popularly known in Nanticoke at that time as "the $5,000 beauty."

The Mowery Fire Company Building at 174 East Noble Street was built in 1912 at a cost of $7,990. With the completion of this new building, the borough council voted in favor of buying a new chemical-and-hose wagon for the Mowery Company, which had been using a hand-pulled hose cart. Mowery vacated this building at the consolidation of all companies at Central Fire Headquarters.

The Nanticoke Hotel at Main and Market Streets gave way to redevelopment in 1969 and was replaced by a Carroll's Drive-in. The building had stood through various owners and uses over the years. Originally built by Louis C. Gabriel, his name can still be seen fixed to the front. The "Polski Adwocat" lettering on the window translates to "Polish Lawyer," the office of attorney Frank L. Groskie.

This building was constructed by the Duplan Silk Manufacturing Company in 1920 and operated until 1951. The McGregor-Doniger Sportswear Company took over the building in 1952 and employed 400 persons, mostly women. At this time, women became the family breadwinners due to the closing of the coal mines, which cost men their jobs. In 1972, McGregor moved this manufacturing operation to Berwick and closed this building.

This postcard view shows a group of nurses at the Nanticoke City Building, located at Broad and Walnut Streets, when it was used as an emergency hospital in 1905. The 1905 typhoid epidemic caused 49 deaths. It was the defining cause for the need of a regular Nanticoke hospital, which was then built in 1909.

The typhoid fever epidemic of 1905 exposed the need for a Nanticoke hospital. Dr. Dixon met with Dr. J.H. Hughes and E.H. Kohlbraker, superintendent of the Susquehanna Coal Company, and discussed the necessity of a hospital. For the site hospital, the Susquehanna Coal Company donated three acres of ground bounded by Grand, Grove, Lincoln, and Lee Mine Streets. It was completed at a cost of $70,000 and dedicated on October 12, 1909.

Samantha Mill's great-grandfather John Mill came to Nanticoke in 1802 and built the Mill Homestead. Samantha, the last surviving member of the Mill family, occupied the Mill Homestead until a few years prior to her death in 1937. The Mill family garnered most of its wealth from extensive land holdings and from the coal deposits it leased to coal mining companies. The Mill Homestead is an example of Georgian and early American design. It was through the generosity of Samantha Mill that the Mill Memorial Library got its start. In her will, Samantha stipulated that the City of Nanticoke be given "the land on which my home is located . . . excepting and reserving land enough for establishing and founding and enlarging a Public Library and near home, a beautiful and suitable library building." The Mill Memorial Library was constructed in 1958 on the plot of ground adjoining the Mill Homestead. The Mill Homestead is home to the offices of the Nanticoke Historical Society. The view of the homestead on this page dates from 1912. (Courtesy of Znaniecki collection.)

While some of the homes in Nanticoke, built by the giants of local industry, were magnificent in all respects, there were less ornate homes built by other people in Nanticoke prior to the turn of the 20th century. This unique home was located at 45–47 West Broad Street. It is noteworthy for its artistic simplicity where form certainly followed function. The owner of the home is the unidentified gentleman pictured on the porch.

The Fairchild family owned massive amounts of land on Nanticoke's west side. In addition, this large family also owned many homes in the Nanticoke area. This Fairchild home was at 182 West Broad Street. (Courtesy of Fairchild collection.)

The Hon home on Main Street in Dewey Park was the first home built in that area. This home was directly across Main Street from the high school. The Znaniecki home on Jifkin Street can be seen in the background of this undated photograph. (Courtesy of Znaniecki collection.)

Dr. Dana W. Kingsbury sits on the porch of his home at 137 State Street. This building also served as his office. This photograph was taken sometime between 1891 and 1910.

Many of the homes in Nanticoke today were built over 100 years ago. They started as basic homes, such as the one pictured here, but over the years, these homes have not only been well maintained but have also been remodeled a number of times.

James F. Shelly, a timber inspector for the Susquehanna Coal Company, built his home at 304 State Street. The location of the home, which was at the intersection of State and Walnut Streets, gave a spectacular view from any of the porches in the area.

This home at 132 East Broad Street was the home of Dr. William B. Stricker until his death in 1919. The following year his widow sold it to Nanticoke hotelman Herman Granitski, who resided there until his death in 1941. In 1948, the home was converted into the Nanticoke VFW and was used as such for many years until membership in the post dwindled and the building was sold. It is now used as an antique store.

House painters are applying a fresh coat to the Janora family residence, located at West Union and Maple Streets. A high degree of maintenance and upkeep has preserved many of these older homes and their inherent charm.

The next four pictures present unusual and unique views of some of the streets in Nanticoke at times when traffic and parking problems did not exist. This is a view of the 100 block of East Broad Street. Note the concrete surface of the roadway. (Author's collection.)

South Market Street in the vicinity of the Grand Street intersection was, like many other streets in Nanticoke, paved with bricks. The brick surface was durable and required little maintenance, such as filling potholes, but was dangerously slippery under any conditions of rain, snow, or even wet leaves. (Author's collection.)

This view of East Main Street, taken from the intersection with Kosciuszko Street, shows a concrete roadway in front of Znaniecki's Gas Station. The State Street School can be seen in the upper portion of this photograph. (Author's collection.)

In a view from in front of the Nanticoke Armory on East Main Street, trolley tracks dominate this photograph. The Nanticoke High School stands on its stately hill in the background, and a wooden picket fence surrounds the Mill Homestead. (Author's collection.)

Hanover Street, just south of the intersection with West Union Street, is a sea of mud from curb to curb in this undated picture of the area. This street would later be paved with bricks.

The streets in the Honey Pot section of Nanticoke were paved in the 1930s but lacked curbing and sidewalks. Along each street was a gutter fabricated of individual stone pieces.

Four

CHURCHES

As one approaches Nanticoke from any direction and takes note of the skyline, one will see the prominence of a number of church steeples. The people of Nanticoke have always been devout church members. In the very early years, religious services were held in individual homes by visiting ministers or priests. The Presbyterians were first organized in the Keithline School, near the intersection of Kosciuszko Street (then Mill Lane) and Middle Road. From those humble beginnings came churches magnificent in structure and features both inside and out. The first wave of immigration to Nanticoke consisted largely of the English and Welsh. They established the first group of churches, including the First Presbyterian (1863), the Welsh Baptist (1871), the Welsh Congregational (1874), the First Methodist (1875), St. George Episcopal (1887), and others.

The second wave of immigration to Nanticoke brought particular ethnic groups. These immigrants established their own churches. Catholicism came to Nanticoke with the Irish, who established St. Francis Church in 1875. The Polish established St. Stanislaus in 1874, and it was the first Polish Catholic church in Luzerne County. St. Joseph's Slovak Church came to be in 1888, and in 1894, Holy Trinity, the largest church in Nanticoke, was formed in the midst of controversy between Polish factions at St. Stanislaus. In 1901, with an overwhelming majority of the population of Nanticoke being of Polish ethnicity, another Polish Catholic church was established as St. Mary's on Hanover Street. St. Joseph's Lithuanian was founded in 1908, St. John's Russian Orthodox in 1911, and St. Nicholas Ukranian Byzantine in 1914.

Family life revolved around one's church. Each Catholic church had its own school, where the children of its members attended the first through eighth grades. School activities were many and varied. Basketball was an integral part of the parochial schools, as each had a team. Competition in these leagues was intense. During the many years of great Nanticoke High School basketball teams, including the state championship team of 1961, much credit was given to the feeder system of the parochial school basketball leagues.

St. Stanislaus was the first Polish Catholic church in Luzerne County. Traveling Polish missionaries who sporadically visited the area ministered to the earliest Polish immigrants. Prior to its establishment in 1874, non-English-speaking Polish Catholics attended St. Nicholas Church in Wilkes-Barre, as many of them spoke the German language that was used there. The Susquehanna Coal Company donated the land on which this church was built. Eventually, the church, shown above in this photograph, was enlarged, and religious classes were held in the basement in 1886. In 1891, the pastor, Reverend Gramlewicz, secured the services of the Sisters of the Holy Family from Chicago and built a convent for them. The sisters were succeeded by the Felician Sisters of Detroit in 1893 and then by the Bernadine Sisters in 1903, who operated the school. In 1925, the steeple was moved from the back to the front of the church, and in 1933, a new school and an auditorium were erected. This church was closed in the realignment of the Scranton Diocese in 2010.

In 1894, a substantial segment of the 2,400 parishioners of St. Stanislaus opted for independence, alleging 17 years of dictatorial rule by Reverend Gramlewicz. On May 1, they organized as the trustees of the new Holy Trinity Congregation and directed their followers to boycott St. Stanislaus and attend St. Joseph's, the Slovak church, until they built their own church only a block away from Reverend Gramlewicz's parish. On September 4, 1894, a plot of ground at Hanover and Ridge Streets was purchased, and construction of Holy Trinity Church was begun. Though first reluctant to do so, Scranton Diocese bishop William O'Hara recognized the existence of Holy Trinity Church and blessed the cornerstone on May 4, 1895. Bishop O'Hara assigned Fr. Francis Hodur as the pastor of Holy Trinity Church. Five different pastors served Holy Trinity between 1897 and 1919. In 1919, Fr. Roman A. Wieziolowski became pastor and served as such for 48 years until he passed away in 1967. The photograph shows the original church, which was replaced in 1931 by the present edifice.

The interior of Holy Trinity Church, the largest in Nanticoke, was elaborately decorated for Christmas in this 1930s picture. Religious holidays were very important and sacred in everyday life. Such was Good Friday, when many of the Catholic miners would not go into the mines on that day. In 1904, a mine accident at the Auchincloss killed 10 miners. The funeral for eight of those miners was held at one time in Holy Trinity Church, and they were all buried together at Holy Trinity Cemetery. (Author's collection.)

This is the original building for the First Methodist Church on Main Street. It was completed in 1880 on land donated by the Susquehanna Coal Company. The completed church cost $8,500 and had 87 members. It was razed in 1915 and the present church edifice was built.

The church that was to become the First Presbyterian Church was organized on November 27, 1829, as the Hanover-Newport Presbyterian Church. The construction of the building pictured was begun in 1893. The prior church was located on the land in the far left of this photograph, currently the site of the manse. (Courtesy of David Shipkowski.)

The interior architecture is shown in this view of the First Presbyterian Church, which was where many of Nanticoke's prominent families worshiped. Donated items are marked with names, such as Fairchild, Mill, Lape, Alexander, Pannebecker, and Thompson. The First Presbyterian Church remains an active and viable asset to Nanticoke. (Author's collection.)

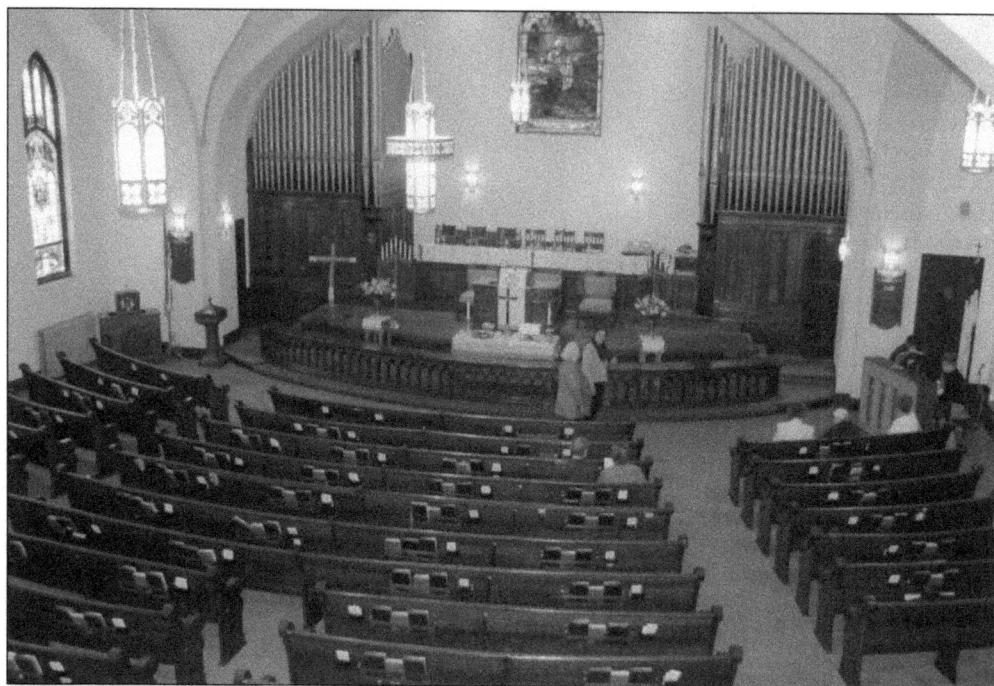

The interior of the First Methodist Church is shown from a balcony view. The morning services are greatly enhanced by the sun shining directly through the stained-glass window, which the congregation faces. It is a portrayal of Christ at prayer in the garden. (Michael Passetti Photograph.)

Here is a similar view of St. John's Lutheran Church at 231 State Street. Founded by early German settlers in Nanticoke, this architectural treasure was dedicated on September 24, 1882, and remains an active part of the Nanticoke community today. (Michael Passetti Photograph.)

As Slovak pioneers began to settle in Nanticoke, they began a fundraising committee to build their own church, St. Joseph's. In 1880, it was completed. The church soon became too small because of the influx of immigrants, and a new church was built at the intersection of Noble and Prospect Streets. It was at this church, pictured here, that the group of Polish Catholics from St. Stanislaus Church worshipped while the new Holy Trinity Church was being built. In the year 2010, all Catholic churches in Nanticoke were consolidated and St. Joseph's Church was closed. The parishioners there then began to attend services at the Holy Trinity Church Building, which was renamed St. Faustina parish.

As the Polish population of Nanticoke continued to grow, St. Mary of Czestachowa Polish Catholic Church was formed in 1901. Their parochial school was located in two rooms in the rear of the church. This wood-framed school was built in 1914, and by 1919, there were 361 students being educated here. A new brick school building was constructed on this site in 1950. In 1967, St. Mary's school was merged with St. Stanislaus School to form Blessed John Newman School. (Courtesy of David Sherrick.)

An example of the individual ethnic church groups is shown in photograph of the Ukranian Dance Group of St. Nicholas Ukranian Church. Their handmade costumes are magnificently detailed with decorations and embellishments brought with them from "the old country."

As seen in this 1916 photograph of the Polish Falcons of Nanticoke, there was no shortage of participation in any of the church-related societies and organizations. A bonus in this photograph is the detail in the architecture in the Pulaski School Building in front of which it was taken. The Polish Falcons owned their own building on Church Street and used it for various organizational and social events.

Five

BARS AND SALOONS

In the September 1913 issue of *Popular Science Monthly*, author G.T. Patrick stated, "Picturing the hopeless grinding toil of the coal miner, his monotonous and unillumined [sic] life, his long day, his hasty and insufficient supper and his hard bed, at the end of the week when respite comes, the 'demand for joy' drives the coal miner to the saloon." An early city directory lists 51 "hotels," 80 saloons, and 6 taverns. These establishments were a large part of daily life in Nanticoke. Many men often went to one of these establishments early in the morning for "an eye opener," and later in the afternoon, some stopped in "to wash the dust down." When money was tight and the men still had to stop by their local bar, they put it on their "tick" bill. That term originates from the bartender placing a small mark or tick on the drinker's beer coaster. When the man got his money on payday, he would go to the bar and pay his tick bill. Many men never made it home with their pay, but left most of it at their local bar. There are tales of women going into the bars and dragging their husbands out. Many times it was the wife of the miner, or sometimes even the miner's priest, who would appear at the coal company's pay office and take the pay so that the family would get it and the miner would not leave the whole pay at the local beer garden.

The culture of alcoholism that permeated Nanticoke and all other towns in Luzerne County, without exception, took many years to fade from the scene. The coal miners used alcohol as an escape mechanism from endless, long hours of backbreaking work underground with no hope of reprieve. As mining faded from the scene and the number of miners dwindled, so did the large number of bars. Bar owners were no longer able to make a living on beer and whiskey sales alone. Their time had come and gone; they had for some, arguably, served their purpose.

The Gross Hotel was at 193 South Market Street, the corner of Market and Broad Streets. It is shown here with the word "Saloon" clearly emblazoned on its front window.

Adam Gapinski operated this saloon on West Ridge Street from around 1891 to 1900. This sign on the beer wagon indicates that it is from the Franklin Brewery in Hanover Township. The sign on the building advertises Susquehanna Beer.

John "Jacenty" Swirat established the Swirat Saloon at 402 Front Street in the Hanover section around 1911. He ran the saloon until 1928; at this time, it was then taken over by his son Joe who ran it for 50 years until his retirement in 1978.

The Coal Mine Tap Room was a very unique place. It had two entrances, this one at 193 South Market Street and another one right around the corner on Broad Street. Both entrances led to stairways that went down to the bar room in the basement of this building. (Norm Borofski Photograph.)

The Rosebush Tavern was one of Nanticoke's best-known establishments. This 1923 facade shows the tavern's swinging door while the signs advertise Nanticoke's Stegmaier beer.

Rosebush owner Casmier Skrzypkowski is tending bar in this 1924 photograph of the interior of his business. His son Charles took over the business in 1927 and added a dining area.

A remodeled exterior and interior of the Rosebush is shown in these photographs. In 1963, Stanley Skrzypkowski and his wife, Helen, took over and ran the bar until it closed in 2000. The building was demolished in July 2003, and the site is now a vacant lot.

This interior design of the Rosebush would prevail until another remodeling in 1936. The exquisite tile floor and the spittoons are noteworthy. Most of the bars and taverns in Nanticoke boasted of elegant fixtures, especially the bar backs. As these businesses closed, these items were highly sought after by dealers and collectors.

In this view of the Coal Mine bar, one can see a part of the "timbered ceiling" decor. At one time, there was an actual mine car loaded with coal in a corner of the room. The Coal Mine Tap Room operated from 1945 until 1984.

The bar area of John Negosh's John's Place, located at 32 North Market Street, shows a strong Art Deco theme. A piano occupies a rear corner, while the doors in the rear on the right lead to the dining area. (Pawlowski Photograph.)

This interior photograph shows the bar area of Sedor's Café, which was destroyed by fire in 1906. That fire must have occurred not long after this picture was taken as the calendar on the wall is a 1906 calendar. The bar originally opened in 1900. (Courtesy of Znaniecki collection.)

Sedor's Café was decorated with flags and bunting for the 1929 Fireman's Association parade. This brick building was constructed in 1908 to replace the former café at this location, which was destroyed by fire in 1906. (Courtesy of Znaniecki collection.)

The Perluke "Hotel" was located at 201 Mosier Street in the Hanover section. George Perluke is shown in this photograph on the extreme right. His wife, Agnes, is to his left and a daughter named Alvina stands on the stoop. The signs affixed to the bar room door advertise Glennon's Beer, which was brewed in Pittston, and Susquehanna Beer, which was brewed in Nanticoke. (Courtesy of William Zaremba.)

In addition to local bars and saloons, many fraternal organizations operated bar rooms for the use of their members. This was the Polish Falcons Hall on Church Street. It was the site of many weddings and major social events. (Courtesy of Znaniecki collection.)

Six

SCHOOLS AND SPORTS

There are many things that create bonds between people. Two of the strongest are schools and sports. In school, it is possible to be with someone from the first through the 12th grade. That would be six hours a day, for 180 days, for 12 years. A person would really get to know another person after that time. The other great bond is sports. Athletes, regardless of the sport, spend many intense moments with each other, in practice, regular games, and in a pursuit of a championship title. So it is and was in Nanticoke. Graduates of the high school, even though they may have been years apart, can share with each other their experiences with perhaps a common teacher or can relate to some nuance of the building. They ask each other if they remember reading the Bible at assembly or singing "The Happy Wanderer" each morning. If a person were there, he would remember; he would understand.

The athletes may share that moment when a long game-winning touchdown run was made or a buzzer-beating basket brought a championship to Nanticoke High School (NHS). Fellow students, not athletes but spectators, will never forget those moments when the whole world revolved around a game.

Is there anyone who was there in 1961 who does not remember the basketball playoff game with Reading when the Nans, down by seven points with two and a half minutes to go, scored 11 straight points to win the game that put them into the state championship?

Schools in any community are always changing. They mostly change on the inside regarding the curriculum but can also change regarding the buildings. This change usually means demolition and new construction, and rightly so, as the children of today deserve the finest in educational surroundings that can be given to them.

The demolition of the Main Street High School generated so much interest that a crowd gathered everyday to watch the "progress." Hundreds of people garnered a brick or two from the old school, which probably now adorn many homes of NHS graduates.

A look back at the schools and some of the greater moments in sports will recall those bonds formed so long ago for some. One might say, "I wonder what ever happened to . . ." or "those were the best years of my life."

The Centennial School was the first brick school in Nanticoke and was built in 1876. It was located at the corner of Noble and Prospect Streets and was situated in the same block as the Pulaski Building. The Pulaski can be seen on the right side of this photograph. Because a large number of young boys were employed in the mines at an early age, few of them attended this school. (Courtesy of Znaniecki collection.)

This large wooden-frame building was constructed in 1891, and initially, the first- through sixth-grade classes were held on the first floor, and the eighth-grade and high school classes were held on the second floor. Seventh-grade classes were conducted in the Centennial School. There were eight classrooms on each floor. By the late 1950s, the school was closed, and the building was razed in 1963.

This imposing brick structure with ornate Roman columns and stonework was the Pulaski Building. Built in 1904, it was the high school building for 10 years. During that time, it was known simply as the high school. When the last class graduated in 1915, it became an elementary school and assumed the Pulaski name. The front of the building was used as a backdrop for many group photographs because of its magnificent architecture. The school was closed because of mine subsidence in 1945 and was razed in 1947. (Courtesy of Znaniecki collection.)

Honey Pot's school building was the Garfield School. A large, white, wooden structure built in 1912, it served the students of that section until the early 1960s.

This is an old classroom in the Kosciuszko Building, which was constructed in 1924 and served mainly as the Nanticoke Junior High or "annex" building. The building housed a large life-sized painting of Thaddeaus Kosciuszko, who assisted the Colonial army during the Revolutionary War. This painting is now kept at the John S. Fine High School. (Courtesy of Znaniecki collection.)

This photograph was taken immediately prior to the demolition of the Washington School, which was closed in 1970. Built in 1893, it served as an auxiliary hospital during the influenza epidemic of 1918. Nothing was rebuilt on the site, and it is now a parking lot for the hospital. (Author's collection.)

This was Nanticoke High School, where "the vale of old Tilbury met the western sky." Built in 1914, it was the high school of more than 10,000 graduates. After the school jointure that resulted in the Greater Nanticoke Area School District, it served as a middle school. It saw its last class in 1995 and fell to the wrecking ball in 1999.

The top of the high school carried the date "1914," and the front doors were topped with simply "High School." Two side front doors were labeled "Boys" and "Girls," a reminder of the early days of the school. (Courtesy of Mike Zaremba.)

Although the building faced Main Street with its primary front doors, these doors were rarely used as access to the school. This was because it was always more convenient to enter the school through the back doors. In its middle school configuration, the main front doors were sealed off, and an office was constructed in that area. (Courtesy of Mike Zaremba.)

On a warm October day in 1999, the end came for the former Nanticoke High School. As dust clouds rose from falling bricks, two large construction vehicles pushed against the steel superstructure from opposite ends. Then, with the groan of bending metal, it fell to the ground. (Author's collection.)

1951

1st Row: Chet Kalinoski, Anastacia Kalinoski (first female), Robert Wisniewski, Joe Kaminski, Joe Augustine, Jack Martin, Greg Sutchko

Standing: John Wisniewski, Team Sponsor, Jack Rasmus, Mike Kwak, Don Komorowski, James Modla, Dan Jacobs (Manager) Clem Sczecinski, Ben Zbrieajewski. Not pictured: Art Gordon

The Nanticoke Little League was organized in 1951 and consisted of four teams: John's Cars, YT Hardware, Honey Pot, and Sheatown. John's Cars, pictured here, won the first Nanticoke Little League Championship.

This 1888 photograph of the Nanticoke Athletic Club's baseball team is typical of the many early amateur baseball teams and baseball clubs.

93

Another amateur baseball team in 1914 was the Nanticoke White Sox, who played in the Philadelphia amateur league. This photograph was most likely taken at Edgewood Park, considering the No. 5 breaker can be seen in the background.

The 1904–1905 Americus basketball team, sponsored by the Knockers Club, was composed of George Powell, Jim O'Brien, Jim Grick, Dave Thomas, Jack Hughes, and Mike Hoar, with Elijah Ellery as equipment manager and Ben Haas as business manager.

There were many amateur basketball teams playing in the many different leagues in the 1920s and 1930s. Unfortunately, sometimes, all that is left behind is a picture without any identification as to the names of the players, team, or league. This is one such photograph of the 1924–1925 E.A.C. basketball team.

The 1937–1938 Nanticoke S.E.U. basketball team poses in this picture with its championship trophy. No other information is known regarding this team.

Nanticoke High School basketball in the 1920s produced memorable teams. After winning the state championship in 1923 by beating Monessen 23-21, this team entered the national playoffs held in Chicago. They beat Montana and then lost to South Carolina. Until the mid-1940s, there had only been one team crowned as state basketball champion. There were no class distinctions between teams.

PENNSYLVANIA STATE CHAMPIONS

Standing—
Left to Right:

SALACK, Faculty Mgr.
BUTKIEWICZ
SHERWOOD
LEARY, Coach
BECKLEY
ESTWANICK
BELL, Student Mgr.

Sitting—

LENTZ
DONOHUE
DOMZALSKI, Capt.
MORGANS
HILL
PRICE

NANTICOKE HIGH SCHOOL BASKETBALL TEAM

The 1926 team won the state championship by beating Erie East 45-22. They took a 28-1 record into the tournament at State College. There they beat in succession Reading, Harrisburg Tech, and then Erie East. They also went on to the national playoffs in Chicago, where they made it all the way to the semifinals by beating Salt Lake City and Wheeler, Mississippi. In the semifinal game, they lost to Fitchburg, Massachusetts.

96

Legendary coach Syl Bozinski is carried off the floor after the 1961 Nanticoke Nans won the PIAA Class A State Championship at the Farm Show Arena in Harrisburg. Players on that team were Ken Legins, Bill James, Richie Kiewlak, George Yanchik, Joe Shepela, Jack Dudrick, Larry Selecky, Gerry Rybak, Robert Grabinski, Duane Ford, Harry Morgan, and Joe Grzymski. Carrying coach Bozinski are Joe Grzymski (closest) and Ken Legins. Joe Shepela is number 23. Class A was the top school classification at the time. The team defeated Hickory Township by the score of 56-46. Coach Bozinski's overall record in 31 years of coaching was 619 wins and 199 losses. His teams won 18 Wyoming Valley Championships, 13 District Two Championships, 9 inter-district playoffs, 2 PIAA Eastern Division Championships, and the 1961 PIAA State Championship. In 1954 and 1955, he was the head football coach and an assistant football coach in 1962 and 1963. Retiring from coaching in 1985, he was affectionately known as "Stretch" to the community, but to his players, he was always "Coach."

A billboard next to the high school on Main Street was painted every year with the upcoming football schedule. After the 1961 basketball team won the state championship, the billboard was painted to reflect that accomplishment. Here, coach Syl Bozinski and assistant coach Norm Groblewski pose with the team at that sign. From left to right are (seated) Jack Dudrick, Joe Shepela, Rick Kiewiak, Duane Ford, Harry Sinco (manager), Larry Selecky, Jerry Rybak, Harry Morgan, Gerry Pegarella, and Joe Grzymski; (standing) George Yanchick, Ken Legins, Bozinski, Groblewski, Bill James, and Bob Grabinski.

The 1990 Nanticoke Area Trojanettes left no doubt that they were the best PIAA girls' basketball team in the state. Undefeated with 30 wins and no losses, coach Rose Volpicelli's team defeated Beaver Falls 77-67 at the Hershey Park Arena. Those pictured are, from left to right, (first row) Nicki Getts, Tia Hornlein, Casey Comoroski, Holly Kozlowski, and Terri Galazin; (second row) Renee Piontkowski, Lori Scally, Ellen Bartuska, JoAnn Opachinski, and Holly Ryncavage. (Courtesy of GNA School District.)

Nanticoke High School was one of the first to field an organized and school-sanctioned team. This 1922 team won the Wyoming Valley Championship. Future high school teams would win Wyoming Valley Football Conference Championships in 1923, 1926, 1928, 1931 (tied), 1932 (tied), 1934, 1937, 1948, 1967, 1968, and 1992. Every year on Thanksgiving Day, Nanticoke and Plymouth would play a football game. The Thanksgiving Day game soon became a part of that holiday's tradition. Fans would go to either Lincoln Field in Nanticoke or Huber Field in Plymouth and watch the Rams battle the Shawnee Indians. Many times, the outcome of this final game of the season resulted in the crowning of the Wyoming Valley Conference champion. For many of these Thanksgiving Day games, it was the norm to have in excess of 10,000 people in attendance. After having played 46 games, the rivalry ended in 1966 due to school consolidation, as Plymouth High School was made a part of the Wyoming Valley West School District.

Nanticoke H. S. Football Squad, Champions of N. E. Penn'a. 1928.

Nanticoke High School's football team, coached by Frank Chicknosky, won the 1928 Northeastern Pennsylvania Football Championship. This team won 11 straight games without a defeat that year. Note in the background of the picture that there is a wooden fence. This fence surrounded the football field, known as Lincoln Field at the time, and would be replaced by a concrete-and-stone wall when the area was rebuilt as Lincoln Stadium.

Another of Frank Chicknosky's championships came with this 1934 team. This team suffered only a 6-0 loss to Coughlin that year, while registering eight shutouts defensively and allowing only 13 other points to be scored against them. In this photograph, the new Lincoln Stadium has been built (1932), and large bleachers and the stone wall can be seen in the background. (Pawlowski Photograph.)

100

Whether Frank Chickson Chicknosky was the Knute Rockne of Nanticoke High School football or Knute Rockne was the Frank Chicknosky of Notre Dame football is still the subject of debate when football fans gather and discuss the glory days of the game. "Chick" was a graduate of Layfayette College where he played football from 1921 to 1924 and was also a heavyweight boxing champion there. As the most successful football coach at Nanticoke High School, he coached for 16 years, from 1925 to 1941. His teams compiled a record of 90 wins, 48 losses, and 12 ties. The second most successful coach was Daniel Distasio whose teams won 71 games, lost 43, and tied 6. The present high school football stadium is named the Frank J. Chicknosky Stadium in his honor.

Lincoln Stadium was built in 1932 on the site of Lincoln Field. The bleachers on each side of the field were 320 feet long and had 12 rows of seats. In this early picture, the field house was not yet built, and the football team dressed and showered in the high school. In 1936, a field house with facilities for both the home and visiting teams was built. It hosted graduation ceremonies, school band concerts, the US Navy Band, and even Golden Gloves boxing tryouts. In or around 1966,

it was decided that a new high school building was needed, and the stadium was selected as the site of the new school. Today, the north-side parking lot occupies most of the old playing field, while the actual high school building begins at the area where fans of the visiting team once sat. (Pawlowski Photograph.)

Pete Gray, the phenomenal one-armed outfielder for the St. Louis Browns, has been the subject of many books and even a television movie. The summer months would find him at the Hanover and Nanticoke little-league fields taking in the games. He never refused an autograph for a young player. A historical marker has been erected along Front Street to commemorate his life. This is the cover of the program from the marker dedication on August 24, 2003. (Courtesy of Pennsylvania Historical and Museum Commission.)

Steve Bilko signed a professional baseball contract with the St. Louis Cardinals in 1945 while he was still a student at Nanticoke High School. He also played for the Los Angeles Angels. During his time in the Pacific Coast League, he was named Most Valuable Player in 1955, 1956, and 1957. During those three years, he hit 148 home runs. In 2003, he was inducted into the Pacific Coast League Hall of Fame. (Courtesy of Michael Zaremba.)

Seven

COAL

The growth of Nanticoke from a village to a borough to a city is due to the anthracite coal industry. Col. Washington Lee was the first to mine coal from the hills of Honey Pot in 1825. Taken from the hillside, it was transported down to the riverbank and loaded onto coal barges for shipment to downstream markets. The first coal breaker that was built by Lee operated from 1852 until 1891. In 1869, the Susquehanna Coal Company purchased Lee's entire holdings, thus beginning one of the most powerful coal companies, which dominated the industry for almost a century. It erected its first breaker in 1870 in Honey Pot and operated it there until 1872. In 1880, breaker No. 5 was erected behind Main Street. Later onto the scene was the DL&W Coal Company, and it erected the Auchincloss and Bliss in 1892 and the Truesdale Colliery in 1903.

As the coal industry was in its infancy, Welsh immigrants came to Nanticoke to drive the shafts for the new mines in the 1840s. As the need for raw labor increased, immigrants from Eastern Europe flocked to this area. The majority of those who settled in Nanticoke consisted of Polish immigrants, with many of them having been recruited by Susquehanna Coal Company agents in New York. Upon their arrival, they would stay with friends or relatives. Later, perhaps, they would obtain company housing where rent was as cheap as $3.50 per month.

Nanticoke suffered a number of catastrophic mine disasters. At the No. 1 Colliery in Honey Pot, 26 men were lost in a rush of water and quicksand in 1885. The bodies of those men were never recovered. A total of 12 men died at No. 7 in an explosion in 1891, and in 1904, eleven were killed at the Auchincloss when a cage fell to the bottom of the shaft. An explosion in 1905 at No. 7 took another seven lives, and in another explosion there, 16 died, including four Novak brothers, in 1920.

By the 1930s, other fuels were being used throughout the country, and anthracite began its decline. In the ensuing years, the jobs faded away and so did the population. Today, Nanticoke is a bedroom community with little or no major employment, except for Luzerne County Community College. The only commercial spaces are used for retail and services for the residents, such as banks, doctors, a grocery supermarket, and pharmacies.

Members of the Nanticoke Historical Society found this photograph in the Susquehanna Coal Company Building on Main Street just prior to its demolition. Based on the men's clothing, it appears to be of the 1890s era. This photograph is most likely of an early work crew of the Susquehanna Coal Company. Attempts to identify the actual operation have been unsuccessful.

This photograph has been dated as 1889 and shows a number of Susquehanna Coal Company surveyors posing with their equipment. The open-flame lights on the hats can determine that this survey crew obviously worked inside of the mines.

A group of younger Susquehanna Coal Company employees poses at the front of a railroad coal car in Honey Pot around 1915. At 11 years of age, boys could work in the mines tending mules that hauled coal cars throughout the mine. Older boys worked as door tenders and mule drivers.

The massive expanse of the Susquehanna No. 7 is evidenced in this photograph showing the colliery from an eastern view. Pennsylvania Railroad coal cars can be seen in the foreground, while others can be seen under the breaker being loaded.

A view of the No. 7 from the west gives a good perspective of the area of the shafts along with the rail yard. Along the right side of this photograph is West Main Street. The intersection with Alden Road is also visible.

The Susquehanna No. 5 stood at the foot of North Market Street until 1922. It was erected in 1880 and dominated the Nanticoke skyline during those years.

Timbers are loaded onto mine cars ready to be taken underground for use in shoring up the roofs of the mines in this photograph of the Susquehanna No. 1.

Here is a wooden mine car in use at the Susquehanna No. 5 in November 1917. Mine cars were moved about in the mines by teams of mules.

An early photograph of the Susquehanna No. 7 operations shows some of the earlier types of railroad coal cars.

The Bliss, a DL&W mine, was started in 1892 and was located on the southern side of Middle Road, immediately before the township line of Nanticoke and Newport. This photograph was taken in 1902.

The Auchincloss was the other DL&W coal mining operation in Nanticoke. It was located at the western side of the intersection of Middle Road and Prospect Street. It was the first coal breaker in the world to be operated by electricity.

The Truesdale, a DL&W mine, was just outside of the Hanover section of Nanticoke in Hanover Township. The breaker suffered a catastrophic fire in 1953, as this postfire picture shows.

Concrete City was built in 1913 as housing for employees of the Truesdale Colliery. There were 22 residences for 40 families. When the first residents moved into their new homes, which rented for $8 a month, there was no central heating, electricity, or hot water. Each home had seven rooms, a living room, dining room, and kitchen on the first floor and four bedrooms on the second. (Courtesy of Robert Janosov.)

When the Glen Alden Coal Company took over the Truesdale Colliery in 1924, Concrete City was abandoned because they did not want to pay to install a sewer line to the complex at a cost of $20,000. In December, the company attempted to dynamite the buildings, but they remained standing despite the use of 100 sticks of dynamite on one structure. The charge required to destroy the buildings would have caused mine subsidence and was considered too risky. (Courtesy of Robert Janosov.)

Eight

THE RIVER

The Susquehanna River gives to, and takes from, the people of Nanticoke. It gave the means for the Nanticoke Indians to come here in their canoes to fish for shad. It gave the early pre–Revolutionary War settlers waterpower to run their gristmills. The river took the coal barges downstream to markets from where it fueled the Industrial Revolution. In the floods of 1936 and 1972, the river brought destruction and misery. In 1972, it took Scalpintown. Today, from time to time, the river brings acid mine water tinged yellow or brown, a remnant of uncontrolled coal mining. But the river, like the city of Nanticoke, fights for its life everyday. More boats are being seen on the river where people are either fishing or just enjoying a nice boat ride, and more men and boys are seen casting a line into its waters. Nanticoke and its river refuse to die, and both are making a comeback.

The river was the only way to transport coal to southern markets, thus construction of the Nanticoke Dam began about 1827. The North Branch Canal, seen in the right of this photograph, facilitated the departure of millions of tons of coal from Nanticoke and the surrounding area. The canal was in operation until 1905, and the Nanticoke Dam faded away during the ensuing years.

On July 13, 1915, Edward Mace drove an overland automobile over the new Nanticoke Bridge, signaling it was open for traffic. Construction of the bridge started in 1914, and the original roadway was constructed of bricks, which concrete later replaced in 1929. Prior to the construction of this bridge by Luzerne County, a number of bridges had been in place over the years that were privately owned with a toll being charged for their use.

One of the previous bridges was a covered bridge, shown in this photograph taken from Honey Pot. The bridge's tollhouse can be seen at the end of the covered portion of the bridge.

This bridge, owned by the Pennsylvania Railroad, carried train and other traffic over the Susquehanna and was also a toll bridge, as the tollhouse can be seen here. The Pennsylvania Railroad raised much opposition to the county's construction of the new bridge, and a court case settled the dispute, which centered around whether or not the new bridge was being built on railroad property.

Though the low-laying Lower Broadway area of Nanticoke was prone to flooding, a number of businesses did operate there. One longtime business, Gabe's Motors, first selling Pontiacs and later selling Dodge cars and trucks, was totally inundated not only in the 1936 flood but also in this the 1972 Hurricane Agnes flood. (Courtesy of Nanticoke Redevelopment Authority.)

The 1972 Hurricane Agnes flood was the beginning of the end of the Lower Broadway or Scalpintown area of Nanticoke. Many homes suffered such extensive damage that they could not be repaired. Some were restored and reoccupied for a period of time, but the federal government purchased the last of the homes in 1978, and the area was cleared. (Courtesy of Nanticoke Redevelopment Authority.)

Nine

TROLLEYS

In some of the earliest photographs of Nanticoke, there always seems to be a trolley present in the picture or it shows the existence of trolley tracks in the middle of the roadway. Trolleys were the mainstay of transportation even as the automobile came onto the scene. Not everyone was able to afford a car, and trolleys filled the bill. The late Edward Miller was a very prolific photographer of trolleys in the Wyoming Valley. Miller took all of the pictures in this chapter. He also filmed the trolleys in color, and his works are available throughout various commercial outlets. Ed would go out everyday and position himself for maybe only one shot. Perhaps, he would get a shot of the Nanticoke Trolley on a certain street one day and would photograph the trolley as it turned onto another street the following day. He was thus able to leave a magnificent record of trolley service and its routes in Wyoming Valley and likewise in Nanticoke. Trolley service for Nanticoke ended on October 16, 1950. For 62 years prior to that, the city had been served by a number of different trolley companies.

This chapter will recreate one of those rides and follow the Nanticoke Trolley as it travels down what is now the Sans Souci Highway; watch it come into Nanticoke, traverse the streets, and the exit the city. As with all historical photographs, what is in the background usually generates as much interest as the main subject.

The interior of a typical trolley car was not a comfortable place for the motorman, as can be seen in this photograph. The placard with the "N" was displayed on the front of the car.

Sans Souci Park was a very popular trolley stop. The park was popular with those of all ages and provided a venue for parties and school picnics. Just to the right of the front of car No. 778, one can see the entrance sign for Sans Souci Park.

Coming down the Sans Souci Parkway, the car arrives at the intersection with Dundee Road. At this point in time, the parkway is still a two-lane road and the trolley tracks parallel the roadway between the Nanticoke city line and Hanover Township.

Pulling away from the Dundee Road intersection, the car continues toward Nanticoke. Throughout this trip, traffic control lights for the trolley line can be seen at some intersections.

The trolley approaches Nanticoke and crosses over the bridge under which the Nanticoke Creek runs. This is the area where the roadway becomes flooded whenever the Susquehanna River reaches flood stage.

Car No. 790 has just passed the State Street intersection. This photograph presents a good view of the large home at 401 East Main Street, which was built by Francis H. Kohlbraker, superintendent of the Susquehanna Coal Company. Kohlbraker served on the Nanticoke School Board and was instrumental in the creation of the Nanticoke State Hospital in 1909.

It looks perhaps that some track work is going on as the car passes the intersection with Spring Street. This is the area of 270 East Main Street, the present location of the Oplinger Towers.

As the car arrives at the Main Street downtown business area, it passes Catnes Chevrolet, the Family Theatre, Stein's Cleaners, and Gayson's Restaurant on the right.

The car has stopped to pick up passengers at the Prospect Street intersection in front of the Singer Sewing Machine Store. Note that work is continuing on the new facade of the Nanticoke National Bank in the background. The fact that the car is traveling into town is shown by the location of the contact pole on top of the car.

This highly detailed photograph has the Nanticoke car a few feet from the end of the line. The Cease Motor Company is in the background, and the tall building on the right is the Keystone Building.

Another older car approaches the end of the Nanticoke line with indication that it connects with Hanover at Summit. Note the row of ventilating windows on the top of this car.

The motorman is out of the car changing the connecting poles on this car. He has just put up the outbound pole and will now recline the inbound side.

Car No. 82 starts the outbound trip. Note that there are no tracks behind the car as this truly is the end of the line. A good view of the Cease Motor Company is shown here, and a glimpse of the Susquehanna Coal Company No. 5 shaft tower can be seen in the background.

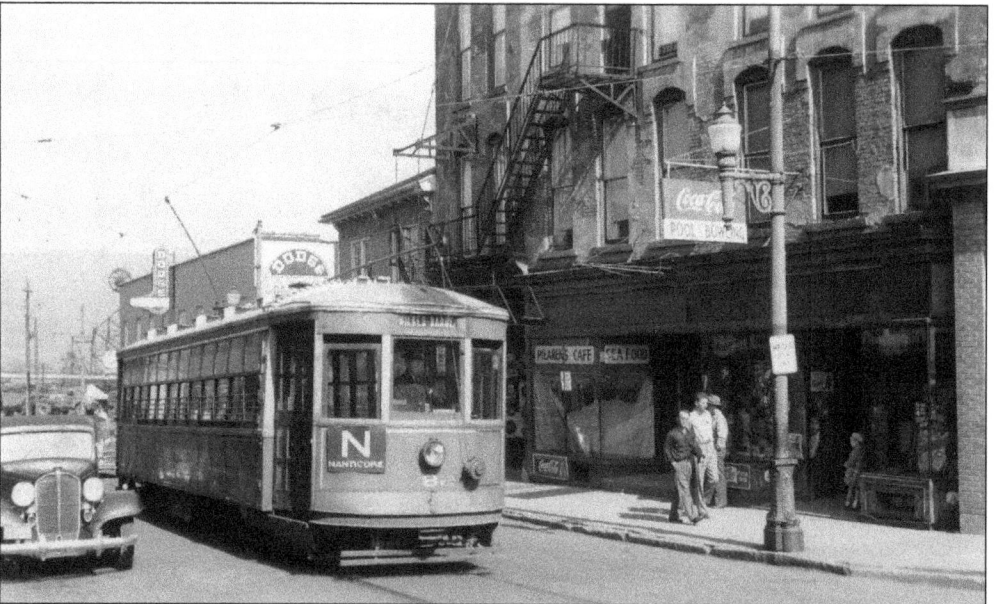

As Car No. 82 approaches the intersection of Main and Market Streets, it is passing Pilarek's Café, which is on the street level of the Keystone Building. Built in 1894, the Keystone was the home of Dreamland, the first moving picture theater in Nanticoke.

The car begins its turn onto Main Street from North Market Street. Diagonal parking was allowed in this area at the time due to the great width of the roadway. The top of the Keystone Building can be seen in this view.

The intersection of Main and Market Streets was the main one in Nanticoke, as can be verified by the slight congestion at the only "red-light" traffic signal in town at the time. The vitality of the city can be seen by the number of businesses at this intersection alone.

While a passenger boards, the motorman adjusts matters on the car in the middle of Main Street. The stately Packard sedan passing the trolley is a harbinger of the coming obsolescence of the trolley system.

Passing the Walnut Street intersection and the front of the Bartuska Furniture Store, this outbound trolley is leaving Nanticoke after a recent snowstorm.

In this photograph, an outbound trolley has actually left the Nanticoke city limits and is in Hanover Township. It is about to cross the Sans Souci Highway from the Loomis Street area and will now run parallel to the highway on its eastbound trip.

Continuing east toward Hanover Township and Wilkes-Barre, the outbound car No. 786 has left Nanticoke, and this journey is over.

Visit us at
arcadiapublishing.com